ODES

Selected by
Ian Hamilton

BLOOMSBURY
★ POETRY ★
CLASSICS

This selection by Ian Hamilton first published 1997
Copyright © 1997 by Bloomsbury Publishing Plc
Bloomsbury Publishing Plc, 38 Soho Square,
London W1V 5DF

A CIP catalogue record for this book
is available from the British Library

ISBN 0 7475 3729 1

10 9 8 7 6 5 4 3 2 1

Typeset in Great Britain by
Hewer Text Composition Services, Edinburgh
Printed in Great Britain by St Edmundsbury Press, Suffolk
Jacket design by Jeff Fisher

CONTENTS

EDMUND SPENSER
Prothalamion

Calm was the day, and through the trembling air
Sweet breathing Zephyrus did softly play,
A gentle spirit, that lightly did delay
Hot Titan's beams, which then did glister fair;
When I whose sullen care,
Through discontent of my long fruitless stay
In prince's court, and expectation vain
Of idle hopes, which still do fly away
Like empty shadows, did afflict my brain,
Walked forth to ease my pain
Along the shore of silver streaming Thames,
Whose rutty bank, the which his river hems,
Was painted all with variable flowers,
And all the meads adorned with dainty gems,
Fit to deck maidens' bowers,
And crown their paramours,
Against the bridal day, which is not long:
   Sweet Thames, run softly, till I end my song.

There, in a meadow, by the river's side,
A flock of nymphs I chanced to espy,
All lovely daughters of the flood thereby,
With goodly greenish locks all loose untied,
As each had been a bride;
And each one had a little wicker basket,
Made of fine twigs entrailed curiously,
In which they gathered flowers to fill their flasket,
And with fine fingers cropped full featously
The tender stalks on high.
Of every sort, which in that meadow grew,
They gathered some; the violet pallid blue,
The little daisy, that at evening closes,
The virgin lily, and the primrose true,
With store of vermeil roses,
To deck their bridegrooms' posies,
Against the bridal day, which was not long:
    Sweet Thames, run softly, till I end my song.

With that, I saw two swans of goodly hue
Come softly swimming down along the Lee;
Two fairer birds I yet did never see.
The snow, which doth the top of Pindus strew,
Did never whiter shew,
Nor Jove himself, when he a swan would be
For love of Leda, whiter did appear:
Yet Leda was they say as white as he,
Yet not so white as these, nor nothing near.
So purely white they were,
That even the gentle stream, the which them bare,
Seemed foul to them, and bade his billows spare
To wet their silken feathers, lest they might
Soil their fair plumes with water not so fair,
And mar their beauties bright,
That shone as heaven's light,
Against their bridal day, which was not long:
    Sweet Thames, run softly, till I end my song.

Eftsoons the nymphs, which now had flowers their fill,
Ran all in haste, to see that silver brood,
As they came floating on the crystal flood.
Whom when they saw, they stood amazed still,
Their wondering eyes to fill.
Them seemed they never saw a sight so fair,
Of fowls so lovely, that they sure did deem
Them heavenly born, or to be that same pair
Which through the sky draw Venus' silver team;
For sure they did not seem
To be begot of any earthly seed,
But rather angels or of angels' breed:
Yet were they bred of Somers-heat they say,
In sweetest season, when each flower and weed
The earth did fresh array,
So fresh they seemed as day,
Even as their bridal day, which was not long:
    Sweet Thames, run softly, till I end my song.

Then forth they all out of their baskets drew
Great store of flowers, the honour of the field,
That to the sense did fragrant odours yield,
All which upon those goodly birds they threw,
And all the waves did strew,
That like old Peneus' waters they did seem,
When down along by pleasant Tempe's shore,
Scattered with flowers, through Thessaly they stream,
That they appear through lilies' plenteous store,
Like a bride's chamber floor.
Two of those nymphs, meanwhile, two garlands
    bound,
Of freshest flowers which in that mead they found,
The which presenting all in trim array,
Their snowy foreheads therewithal they crowned,
Whilst one did sing this lay,
Prepared against that day,
Against their bridal day, which was not long:
    Sweet Thames, run softly, till I end my song.

'Ye gentle birds, the world's fair ornament,
And heaven's glory, whom this happy hour
Doth lead unto your lovers' blissful bower,
Joy may you have and gentle heart's content
Of your love's couplement:
And let fair Venus, that is queen of love,
With her heart-quelling son upon you smile,
Whose smile, they say, hath virtue to remove
All love's dislike, and friendship's faulty guile
For ever to assoil.
Let endless peace your steadfast hearts accord,
And blessed plenty wait upon your board,
And let your bed with pleasures chaste abound,
That fruitful issue may to you afford,
Which may your foes confound,
And make your joys redound,
Upon your bridal day, which is not long:
    Sweet Thames, run softly, till I end my song.'

So ended she; and all the rest around
To her redoubled that her undersong,
Which said, their bridal day should not be long.
And gentle echo from the neighbour ground
Their accents did resound.
So forth those joyous birds did pass along,
Adown the Lee, that to them murmured low,
As he would speak, but that he lacked a tongue,
Yet did by signs his glad affection show,
Making his stream run slow.
And all the fowl which in his flood did dwell
'Gan flock about these twain, that did excel
The rest so far as Cynthia doth shend
The lesser stars. So they, enranged well,
Did on those two attend,
And their best service lend,
Against their wedding day, which was not long:
   Sweet Thames, run softly, till I end my song.

At length they all to merry London came,
To merry London, my most kindly nurse,
That to me gave this life's first native source;
Though from another place I take my name,
An house of ancient fame.
There when they came, whereas those bricky towers,
The which on Thames' broad aged back do ride,
Where now the studious lawyers have their bowers
There whilom wont the Templar Knights to bide,
Till they decayed through pride:
Next whereunto there stands a stately place,
Where oft I gained gifts and goodly grace
Of that great lord, which therein wont to dwell,
Whose want too well now feels my friendless case.
But ah! here fits not well
Old woes but joys to tell
Against the bridal day, which is not long:
    Sweet Thames, run softly, till I end my song.

Yet therein now doth lodge a noble peer,
Great England's glory and the world's wide wonder,
Whose dreadful name late through all Spain did
  thunder,
And Hercules' two pillars standing near
Did make to quake and fear.
Fair branch of honour, flower of chivalry,
That fillest England with thy triumph's fame,
Joy have thou of thy noble victory,
And endless happiness of thine own name
That promiseth the same:
That through thy prowess and victorious arms,
Thy country may be freed from foreign harms;
And great Elisa's glorious name may ring
Through all the world, filled with thy wide alarms,
Which some brave Muse may sing
To ages following,
Upon the bridal day, which is not long:
    Sweet Thames, run softly, till I end my song.

From those high towers this noble lord issuing,
Like radiant Hesper when his golden hair
In th' Ocean billows he hath bathed fair,
Descended to the river's open viewing,
With a great train ensuing.
Above the rest were goodly to be seen
Two gentle knights of lovely face and feature
Beseeming well the bower of any queen,
With gifts of wit and ornaments of nature,
Fit for so goodly stature;
That like the twins of Jove they seemed in sight,
Which deck the baldric of the heavens bright.
They two forth pacing to the river's side,
Received those two fair birds, their love's delight,
Which at th'appointed tide
Each one did make his bride,
Against their bridal day, which is not long:
    Sweet Thames, run softly, till I end my song.

JOHN MILTON
On the Morning of Christ's Nativity

I

This is the month, and this the happy morn
Wherein the Son of Heaven's eternal King,
Of wedded maid and virgin mother born,
Our great redemption from above did bring;
For so the holy sages once did sing,
 That he our deadly forfeit should release,
And with his Father work us a perpetual peace.

II

That glorious form, that light unsufferable,
And that far-beaming blaze of majesty,
Wherewith he wont at Heaven's high council-table
To sit the midst of Trinal Unity,
He laid aside; and here with us to be,
 Forsook the courts of everlasting day,
And chose with us a darksome house of mortal clay.

III

Say Heavenly Muse, shall not thy sacred vein
Afford a present to the Infant God?
Hast thou no verse, no hymn, or solemn strain,
To welcome him to this his new abode,
Now while the heaven, by the sun's team untrod,
 Hath took no print of the approaching light,
And all the spangled host keep watch in squadrons
 bright?

IV

See how from far upon the eastern road
The star-led wizards haste with odours sweet.
O run, prevent them with thy humble ode,
And lay it lowly at his blessed feet;
Have thou the honour first thy Lord to greet,
    And join thy voice unto the Angel quire
From out his secret altar toucht with hallowed fire.

The Hymn
I

It was the winter wild,
While the Heaven-born child
All meanly wrapt in the rude manger lies;
Nature in awe to him
Had doffed her gaudy trim,
With her great Master so to sympathize:
It was no season then for her
To wanton with the sun, her lusty paramour.

II

Only with speeches fair
She woos the gentle air
To hide her guilty front with innocent snow,
And on her naked shame,
Pollute with sinful blame,
The saintly veil of maiden white to throw,
Confounded that her Maker's eyes
Should look so near upon her foul deformities.

III

But he her fears to cease,
Sent down the meek-eyed Peace,
She crowned with olive green came softly sliding
Down through the turning sphere
His ready harbinger,
With turtle wing the amorous clouds dividing,
And waving wide her myrtle wand
She strikes a universal peace through sea and land.

IV

No war, or battle's sound
Was heard the World around,
The idle spear and shield were high up hung;
The hooked chariot stood
Unstained with hostile blood,
The trumpet spake not to the armed throng;
And kings sat still with awful eye,
As if they surely knew their sovereign lord was by.

V

But peaceful was the night
Wherein the Prince of light
His reign of peace upon the earth began.
The winds with wonder whist
Smoothly the waters kissed,
Whispering new joys to the mild Ocean,
Who now hath quite forgot to rave,
While birds of calm sit brooding on the charmed wave.

VI

The stars with deep amaze
Stand fixed in steadfast gaze,
Bending one way their precious influence,
And will not take their flight,
For all the morning light,
Or Lucifer that often warned them thence;
But in their glimmering orbs did glow,
Until their Lord himself bespake and bid them go.

VII

And though the shady gloom
Had given day her room,
The sun himself withheld his wonted speed,
And hid his head for shame,
As his inferior flame
The new enlightened world no more should need;
He saw a greater sun appear
Than his bright throne or burning axletree could bear.

VIII

The shepherds on the lawn,
Or ere the point of dawn,
Sat simply chatting in a rustic row;
Full little thought they then
That the mighty Pan
Was kindly come to live with them below;
Perhaps their loves, or else their sheep,
Was all that did their silly thoughts so busy keep.

IX

When such music sweet
Their hearts and ears did greet,
As never was by mortal finger strook,
Divinely-warbled voice
Answering the stringed noise,
As all their souls in blissful rapture took.
The air such pleasure loth to lose
With thousand echoes still prolongs each heavenly close.

X

Nature that heard such sound
Beneath the hollow round
Of Cynthia's seat the airy region thrilling,
Now was almost won
To think her part was done
And that her reign had here its last fulfilling;
She knew such harmony alone
Could hold all Heaven and Earth in happier union.

XI

At last surrounds their sight
A globe of circular light,
That with long beams the shamed-faced night arrayed;
The helmed cherubim
And sworded seraphim
Are seen in glittering ranks with wings displayed,
Harping in loud and solemn quire
With unexpressive notes to Heaven's new-born heir.

XII

Such music (as 'tis said)
Before was never made,
But when of old the sons of morning sung,
While the Creator great
His constellations set,
And the well-balanced world on hinges hung,
And cast the dark foundations deep,
And bid the weltering waves their oozy channel keep.

XIII

Ring out ye crystal spheres,
Once bless our human ears
(If ye have power to touch our senses so)
And let your silver chime
Move in melodious time;
And let the bass of Heaven's deep organ blow,
And with your ninefold harmony
Make up full consort to th'angelic symphony.

XIV

For if such holy song
Enwrap our fancy long,
Time will run back, and fetch the age of gold,
And speckled vanity
Will sicken soon and die,
And leprous sin will melt from earthly mould,
And Hell itself will pass away,
And leave her dolorous mansions to the peering day.

XV

Yea truth and justice then
Will down return to men,
Orbed in a rainbow; and like glories wearing
Mercy will sit between
Throned in celestial sheen,
With radiant feet the tissued clouds down steering,
And Heaven as at some festival,
Will open wide the gates of her high palace hall.

XVI

But wisest Fate says no,
This must not yet be so,
The babe lies yet in smiling infancy,
That on the bitter cross
Must redeem our loss;
So both himself and us to glorify.
Yet first to those ychained in sleep
The wakeful trump of doom must thunder through the deep,

XVII

With such a horrid clang
As on Mount Sinai rang
While the red fire and smouldering clouds out brake.
The aged earth aghast
With terror of that blast
Shall from the surface to the centre shake,
When at the world's last session
The dreadful Judge in middle air shall spread his throne.

XVIII

And then at last our bliss
Full and perfect is,
But now begins; for from this happy day
Th'old dragon underground
In straiter limits bound,
Not half so far casts his usurped sway,
And wrath to see his kingdom fail
Swindges the scaly horror of his folded tail.

XIX

The oracles are dumb,
No voice or hideous hum
Runs through the arched roof in words deceiving.
Apollo from his shrine
Can no more divine,
With hollow shriek the steep of Delphos leaving.
No nightly trance, or breathed spell,
Inspires the pale-eyed priest from the prophetic cell.

XX

The lonely mountains o'er,
And the resounding shore,
A voice of weeping heard and loud lament;
From haunted spring, and dale
Edged with poplar pale,
The parting genius is with sighing sent;
With flower-inwoven tresses torn
The nymphs in twilight shade of tangled thickets mourn.

XXI

In consecrated earth,
And on the holy hearth,
The Lars and Lemures moan with midnight plaint,
In urns and altars round,
A drear and dying sound
Affrights the flamens at their service quaint;
And the chill marble seems to sweat,
While each peculiar power forgoes his wonted seat.

XXII

Peor and Baalim
Forsake their temples dim,
With that twice-battered god of Palestine,
And mooned Ashtaroth,
Heaven's queen and mother both,
Now sits not girt with tapers' holy shine;
The Libyc Hammon shrinks his horn,
In vain the Tyrian maids their wounded Thammuz mourn.

XXIII

And sullen Moloch fled,
Hath left in shadows dread
His burning idol all of blackest hue;
In vain with cymbals' ring
They call the grisly king,
In dismal dance about the furnace blue;
The brutish gods of Nile as fast,
Isis and Orus and the dog Anubis haste.

XXIV

Nor is Osiris seen
In Memphian grove or green,
Trampling the unshowered grass with lowings loud;
Nor can he be at rest
Within his sacred chest,
Nought but profoundest Hell can be his shroud;
In vain with timbrelled anthems dark
The sable-stoled sorcerers bear his worshipped ark.

XXV

He feels from Juda's land
The dreaded infant's hand,
The rays of Bethlehem blind his dusky eyn;
Nor all the gods beside
Longer dare abide,
Not Typhon huge ending in snaky twine.
Our babe to show his godhead true
Can in his swaddling bands control the damned crew.

XXVI

So when the sun in bed,
Curtained with cloudy red,
Pillows his chin upon an orient wave,
The flocking shadows pale
Troop to th'infernal jail,
Each fettered ghost slips to his several grave,
And the yellow-skirted fays
Fly after the night-steeds, leaving their moon-loved maze.

But see the Virgin blest
Hath laid her babe to rest.
Time is our tedious song should here have ending;
Heaven's youngest teemed star
Hath fixed her polished car,
Her sleeping Lord with handmaid lamp attending;
And all about the courtly stable
Bright-harnessed angels sit in order serviceable.

ANDREW MARVELL
An Horation Ode upon Cromwell's Return from Ireland

The forward youth that would appear
Must now forsake his muses dear,
  Nor in the shadows sing
  His numbers languishing.
'Tis time to leave the books in dust,
And oil the unusèd armour's rust:
  Removing from the wall
  The corslet of the hall.
So restless Cromwell could not cease
In the inglorious arts of peace,
  But through adventurous war
  Urgèd his active star.
And, like the three-forked lightning, first
Breaking the clouds where it was nursed,
  Did thorough his own side
  His fiery way divide.
(For 'tis all one to courage high
The emulous or enemy:
  And with such to inclose
  Is more than to oppose.)

Then burning through the air he went,
And palaces and temples rent:
    And Caesar's head at last
    Did through his laurels blast.
'Tis madness to resist or blame
The force of angry heaven's flame:
    And, if we would speak true,
    Much to the man is due,
Who, from his private gardens, where
He lived reservèd and austere,
    As if his highest plot
    To plant the bergamot,
Could by industrious valour climb
To ruin the great work of time,
    And cast the kingdoms old
    Into another mould.
Though justice against fate complain,
And plead the ancient rights in vain:
    But those do hold or break
    As men are strong or weak.
Nature, that hateth emptiness,
Allows of penetration less:
    And therefore must make room
    Where greater spirits come.

What field of all the Civil Wars,
Where his were not the deepest scars?
   And Hampton shows what part
   He had of wiser art,
Where, twining subtle fears with hope,
He wove a net of such a scope,
   That Charles himself might chase
   To Carisbrooke's narrow case:
That thence the royal actor born
The tragic scaffold might adorn:
   While round the armèd bands
   Did clap their bloody hands.
He nothing common did or mean
Upon that memorable scene:
   But with his keener eye
   The axe's edge did try:
Nor called the gods with vulgar spite
To vindicate his helpless right,
   But bowed his comely head,
   Down, as upon a bed.
This was that memorable hour
Which first assured the forcèd power.
   So when they did design
   The Capitol's first line,

A bleeding head where they begun,
Did fright the architects to run;
   And yet in that the State
   Foresaw its happy fate.
And now the Irish are ashamed
To see themselves in one year tamed:
   So much one man can do,
   That does both act and know.
They can affirm his praises best,
And have, though overcome, confessed
   How good he is, how just,
   And fit for highest trust:
Nor yet grown stiffer with command,
But still in the Republic's hand:
   How fit he is to sway
   That can so well obey.
He to the Commons' feet presents
A kingdom, for his first year's rents:
   And, what he may, forbears
   His fame, to make it theirs:
And has his sword and spoils ungirt,
To lay them at the public's skirt.
   So when the falcon high
   Falls heavy from the sky,

She, having killed, no more does search
But on the next green bough to perch,
    Where, when he first does lure,
    The falc'ner has her sure.
What may not then our isle presume
While Victory his crest does plume?
    What may not others fear
    If thus he crowns each year?
A Caesar, he, ere long to Gaul,
To Italy an Hannibal,
    And to all states not free
    Shall climactéric be.
The Pict no shelter now shall find
Within his parti-coloured mind,
    But from this valour sad
    Shrink underneath the plaid:
Happy, if in the tufted brake
The English hunter him mistake,
    Nor lay his hounds in near
    The Caledonian deer.
But thou, the Wars' and Fortune's son,
March indefatigably on,
    And for the last effect
    Still keep thy sword erect:
Besides the force it has to fright
The spirits of the shady night,
    The same arts that did gain
    A power, must it maintain.

JOHN DRYDEN
A Song for St Cecilia's Day, 1687

I

From harmony, from heavenly harmony,
    This universal frame began:
  When nature underneath a heap
    Of jarring atoms lay,
  And could not heave her head,
The tuneful voice was heard from high,
    'Arise, ye more than dead.'
Then cold, and hot, and moist, and dry,
In order to their stations leap,
    And Music's power obey.
From harmony, from heavenly harmony,
    This universal frame began;
    From harmony to harmony
Through all the compass of the notes it ran,
The diapason closing full in man.

II

What passion cannot music raise and quell?
    When Jubal struck the corded shell,
  His listening brethren stood around,
  And, wondering, on their faces fell
  To worship that celestial sound:
Less than a God they thought there could not dwell
    Within the hollow of that shell
    That spoke so sweetly and so well.
What passion cannot music raise the quell?

III

The trumpet's loud clangour
 Excites us to arms,
With shrill notes of anger
 And mortal alarms.
The double double double beat
 Of the thundering drum,
Cries 'hark! the foes come:
Charge, charge! 'tis too late to retreat.'

IV

The soft complaining flute,
In dying notes discovers
The woes of hopeless lovers;
Whose dirge is whispered by the warbling lute.

V

Sharp violins proclaim
Their jealous pangs, and desperation,
Fury, frantic indignation,
Depth of pains, and height of passion,
 For the fair, disdainful dame.

VI

But, oh! what art can teach,
 What human voice can reach,
The sacred organ's praise?
Notes inspiring holy love,
Notes that wing their heavenly ways
 To mend the choirs above.

VII

Orpheus could lead the savage race;
And trees unrooted left their place,
    Sequacious of the lyre:
But bright Cecilia raised the wonder higher;
When to her organ vocal breath was given,
An angel heard, and straight appeared,
    Mistaking earth for heaven.

Grand Chorus

As from the power of sacred lays
    The spheres began to move,
And sung the great creator's praise
    To all the blessed above;
So when the last and dreadful hour
This crumbling pageant shall devour,
The trumpet shall be heard on high,
The dead shall live, the living die,
And Music shall untune the sky.

JOHN DRYDEN
An Ode on the Death of Mr Henry Purcell

I

Mark how the lark and linnet sing;
        With rival notes
    They strain their warbling throats,
        To welcome in the spring.
        But in the close of night,
    When Philomel begins her heavenly lay,
        They cease their mutual spite,
        Drink in her music with delight,
And, listening and silent and silent and listening,
        and listening and silent obey.

II

So ceased the rival crew when Purcell came;
They sang no more, or only sang his fame.
Struck dumb, they all admired the godlike man:
        The goodlike man,
        Alas! too soon retired,
        As he too late began.
We beg not hell our Orpheus to restore;
    Had he been there,
    Their sovereigns' fear
    Had sent him back before.
The power of harmony too well they know:
He long ere this had tuned their jarring sphere,
        And left no hell below.

III

   The heavenly choir, who heard his notes from high,
   Let down the scale of music from the sky;
      They handed him along,
And all the way he taught, and all the way they sung.
   Ye brethren of the lyre, and tuneful voice,
   Lament his lot, but at your own rejoice:
   Now live secure, and linger out your days;
   The gods are pleased alone with Purcell's lays,
      Nor know to mend their choice.

WILLIAM COLLINS
Ode Written in MDCCXLVI

How sleep the Brave who sink to rest
By all their Country's wishes blest!
When Spring, with dewy fingers cold,
Returns to deck their hallow'd mould,
She there shall dress a sweeter sod
Than Fancy's feet have ever trod.

By fairy hands their knell is rung,
By forms unseen their dirge is sung:
There Honour comes, a pilgrim grey,
To bless the turf that wraps their clay;
And Freedom shall awhile repair
To dwell a weeping hermit there!

THOMAS GRAY
Ode on the Spring

Lo! where the rosy-bosomed Hours,
   Fair Venus' train, appear,
Disclose the long-expecting flowers
   And wake the purple year!
The Attic warbler pours her throat
Responsive to the cuckoo's note,
The untaught harmony of Spring:
   While, whispering pleasure as they fly,
   Cool Zephyrs through the clear blue sky
Their gathered fragrance fling.

Where'er the oak's thick branches stretch
   A broader, browner shade,
Where'er the rude and moss-grown beech
   O'er-canopies the glade,
Beside some water's rushy brink
With me the Muse shall sit, and think
(At ease reclined in rustic state)
   How vain the ardour of the Crowd;
   How low, how little are the Proud,
How indigent the Great!

Still is the toiling hand of Care;
   The panting herds repose:
Yet hark, how through the peopled air
   The busy murmur glows!

39

The insect youth are on the wing,
Eager to taste the honied spring
And float amid the liquid noon:
    Some lightly o'er the current skim,
    Some show their gaily-gilded trim
Quick-glancing to the sun.

To Contemplation's sober eye
    Such is the race of Man:
And they that creep, and they that fly,
    Shall end where they began.
Alike the busy and the gay
But flutter through life's little day,
In Fortune's varying colours dressed:
    Brushed by the hand of rough Mischance,
    Or chilled by Age, their airy dance
They leave, in dust to rest.

Methinks I hear in accents low
    The sportive kind reply:
Poor moralist! and what art thou?
    A solitary fly!
Thy joys no glittering female meets,
No hive hast thou of hoarded sweets,
No painted plumage to display:
    On hasty wings thy youth is flown;
    Thy sun is set, thy spring is gone –
We frolic while 'tis May.

THOMAS GRAY
Ode on a Distant Prospect of Eton College

Ye distant spires, ye antique towers
  That crown the watery glade,
Where grateful Science still adores
  Her Henry's holy shade;
And ye, that from the stately brow
Of Windsor's heights th' expanse below
  Of grove, of lawn, of mead survey,
Whose turf, whose shade, whose flowers among
Wanders the hoary Thames along
  His silver-winding way:

Ah happy hills! ah pleasing shade!
  Ah fields beloved in vain!
Where once my careless childhood strayed,
  A stranger yet to pain!
I feel the gales that from ye blow
A momentary bliss bestow,
  As waving fresh their gladsome wing
My weary soul they seem to soothe,
And, redolent of joy and youth,
  To breathe a second spring.

Say, Father Thames, for thou hast seen
  Full many a sprightly race
Disporting on thy margent green
  The paths of pleasure trace;

Who foremost now delight to cleave
With pliant arm, thy glassy wave?
   The captive linnet which enthral?
What idle progeny succeed
To chase the rolling circle's speed
   Or urge the flying ball?

While some on earnest business bent
   Their murmuring labours ply
'Gainst graver hours, that bring constraint
   To sweeten liberty:
Some bold adventurers disdain
The limits of their little reign
   And unknown regions dare descry:
Still as they run they look behind,
They hear a voice in every wind,
   And snatch a fearful joy.

Gay hope is theirs by fancy fed,
   Less pleasing when possest;
The tear forgot as soon as shed,
   The sunshine of the breast:
Theirs buxom health, of rosy hue,
Wild wit, invention ever new,
   And lively cheer, of vigour born;
The thoughtless day, the easy night,
The spirits pure, the slumbers light
   That fly th' approach of morn.

Alas! regardless of their doom
    The little victims play!
No sense have they of ills to come
    Nor care beyond to-day:
Yet see how all around them wait
The Ministers of human fate
    And black Misfortune's baleful train!
Ah show them where in ambush stand
To seize their prey, the murderous band!
    Ah, tell them they are men!

These shall the fury Passions tear,
    The vultures of the mind,
Disdainful Anger, pallid Fear,
    And Shame that skulks behind,
Or pining Love shall waste their youth;
Or Jealousy with rankling tooth
    That inly gnaws the secret heart,
And Envy wan, and faded Care,
Grim-visaged comfortless Despair,
    And Sorrow's piercing dart.

Ambition this shall tempt to rise,
    Then whirl the wretch from high,
To bitter Scorn a sacrifice
    And grinning Infamy.
The stings of Falsehood those shall try,
And hard Unkindness' altered eye,
    That mocks the tear it forced to flow;

And keen Remorse with blood defiled,
And moody Madness laughing wild
    Amid severest woe.

Lo, in the vale of years beneath
    A griesly troop are seen,
The painful family of Death,
    More hideous than their Queen:
This racks the joints, this fires the veins,
That every labouring sinew strains,
    Those in the deeper vitals rage:
Lo, Poverty, to fill the band,
That numbs the soul with icy hand,
    And slow-consuming Age.

To each his sufferings: all are men;
    Condemned alike to groan;
The tender for another's pain,
    Th' unfeeling for his own.
Yet, ah! why should they know their fate,
Since sorrow never comes too late,
    And happiness too swiftly flies?
Thought would destroy their paradise.
No more; – where ignorance is bliss,
    'Tis folly to be wise.

WILLIAM WORDSWORTH

*Ode: Intimations of Immortality from Recollections of
Early Childhood*

The Child is father of the Man;
And I could wish my days to be
Bound each to each by natural piety.

I

There was a time when meadow, grove, and stream,
The earth, and every common sight,
     To me did seem
     Apparelled in celestial light,
The glory and the freshness of a dream.
It is not now as it hath been of yore; –
     Turn wheresoe'er I may,
         By night or day,
The things which I have seen I now can see no more.

II

     The Rainbow comes and goes,
     And lovely is the Rose,
     The Moon doth with delight
Look round her when the heavens are bare,

Waters on a starry night
　　Are beautiful and fair;
　The sunshine is a glorious birth;
　But yet I know, where'er I go,
That there hath past away a glory from the earth.

III

Now, while the birds thus sing a joyous song,
　　And while the young lambs bound
　　　As to the tabor's sound,
To me alone there came a thought of grief:
A timely utterance gave that thought relief,
　　And I again am strong:
The cataracts blow their trumpets from the steep;
No more shall grief of mine the season wrong;
I hear the Echoes through the mountains throng,
The Winds come to me from the fields of sleep,
　　And all the earth is gay;
　　　Land and sea
　Give themselves up to jollity,
　　And with the heart of May
Doth every Beast keep holiday; –
　　Thou Child of Joy,
Shout round me, let me hear thy shouts, thou happy
　Shepherd-boy!

Ye blessèd Creatures, I have heard the call
   Ye to each other make; I see
The heavens laugh with you in your jubilee;
   My heart is at your festival,
     My head hath its coronal,
The fulness of your bliss, I feel – I feel it all.
     Oh evil day! if I were sullen
     While Earth herself is adorning,
      This sweet May-morning,
     And the Children are culling
      On every side,
     In a thousand valleys far and wide,
     Fresh flowers; while the sun shines warm,
And the Babe leaps up on his Mother's arm:–
     I hear, I hear, with joy I hear!
     – But there's a Tree, of many, one,
A single Field which I have looked upon,
Both of them speak of something that is gone:
     The Pansy at my feet
     Doth the same tale repeat:
Whither is fled the visionary gleam?
Where is it now, the glory and the dream?

V

Our birth is but a sleep and a forgetting:
The Soul that rises with us, our life's Star,
    Hath had elsewhere its setting,
      And cometh from afar:
    Not in entire forgetfulness,
    And not in utter nakedness,
But trailing clouds of glory do we come
    From God, who is our home:
Heaven lies about us in our infancy!
Shades of the prison-house begin to close
    Upon the growing Boy
But He beholds the light, and whence it flows,
    He sees it in his joy;
The Youth, who daily farther from the east
    Must travel, still is Nature's Priest,
      And by the vision splendid
      Is on his way attended;
At length the Man perceives it die away,
And fade into the light of common day.

VI

Earth fills her lap with pleasures of her own;
Yearnings she hath in her own natural kind,
And, even with something of a Mother's mind,
    And no unworthy aim,
    The homely Nurse doth all she can
To make her Foster-child, her Inmate Man,
    Forget the glories he hath known,
And that imperial palace whence he came.

VII

Behold the Child among his new-born blisses,
A six years' Darling of a pigmy size!
See, where 'mid work of his own hand he lies,
Fretted by sallies of his mother's kisses,
With light upon him from his father's eyes!
See, at his feet, some little plan or chart,
Some fragment from his dream of human life,
Shaped by himself with newly-learned art;

    A wedding or a festival,

    A mourning or a funeral;

      And this hath now his heart,

    And unto this he frames his song:

      Then will he fit his tongue

To dialogues of business, love, or strife;

    But it will not be long

    Ere this be thrown aside,

    And with new joy and pride

The little Actor cons another part;
Filling from time to time his 'humorous stage'
With all the Persons, down to palsied Age,
That Life brings with her in her equipage;

    As if his whole vocation

    Were endless imitation.

VIII

Thou, whose exterior semblance doth belie
    Thy Soul's immensity;
Thou best Philosopher, who yet dost keep
Thy heritage, thou Eye among the blind,
That, deaf and silent, read'st the eternal deep,
Haunted for ever by the eternal mind, –
    Mighty Prophet! Seer blest!
    On whom those truths do rest,
Which we are toiling all our lives to find,
In darkness lost, the darkness of the grave;
Thou, over whom thy Immortality
Broods like the Day, a Master o'er a Slave,
A Presence which is not to be put by;
    To whom the grave
Is but a lonely bed without the sense or sight
    Of day or the warm light,
A place of thought where we in waiting lie;
Thou little Child, yet glorious in the might
Of heaven-born freedom on thy being's height,
Why with such earnest pains dost thou provoke
The years to bring the inevitable yoke,
Thus blindly with thy blessedness at strife?
Full soon thy Soul shall have her earthly freight,
And custom lie upon thee with a weight,
Heavy as frost, and deep almost as life!

IX

O joy! that in our embers
Is something that doth live,
That nature yet remembers
What was so fugitive!
The thought of our past years in me doth breed
Perpetual benediction: not indeed
For that which is most worthy to be blest;
Delight and liberty, the simple creed
Of Childhood, whether busy or at rest,
With new-fledged hope still fluttering in his breast: –
      Not for these I raise
      The song of thanks and praise;
   But for those obstinate questionings
   Of sense and outward things,
   Fallings from us, vanishings;
   Blank misgivings of a Creature
Moving about in worlds not realised,
High instincts before which our mortal Nature
Did tremble like a guilty Thing surprised;
      But for those first affections,
      Those shadowy recollections,
   Which, be they what they may,
Are yet the fountain-light of all our day,

Are yet a master-light of all our seeing;
  Uphold us, cherish, and have power to make
Our noisy years seem moments in the being
Of the eternal Silence: truths that wake,
    To perish never:
Which neither listlessness, nor mad endeavour,
    Nor Man nor Boy,
Nor all that is at enmity with joy,
Can utterly abolish or destroy!
  Hence in a season of calm weather
    Though inland far we be,
Our Souls have sight of that immortal sea
    Which brought us hither,
  Can in a moment travel thither,
And see the Children sport upon the shore,
And hear the mighty waters rolling evermore.

SAMUEL TAYLOR COLERIDGE
Dejection: An Ode

> Late, late yestreen I saw the new Moon,
>   With the old Moon in her arms;
> And I fear, I fear, My Master dear!
>   We shall have a deadly storm.
>   *Ballad of Sir Patrick Spence*

I

Well! If the Bard was weather-wise, who made
    The grand old ballad of Sir Patrick Spence,
    This night, so tranquil now, will not go hence
Unroused by winds, that ply a busier trade
Than those which mould yon cloud in lazy flakes,
Or the dull sobbing draft, that moans and rakes
Upon the strings of this Aeolian lute,
        Which better far were mute.
    For lo! the New-moon winter-bright!
    And overspread with phantom light,
    (With swimming phantom light o'erspread
    But rimmed and circled by a silver thread)
I see the old Moon in her lap, foretelling
    The coming on of rain and squally blast.
And oh! that even now the gust were swelling,
    And the slant night-shower driving loud and fast!
Those sounds which oft have raised me, whilst they
  awed,
        And sent my soul abroad,

54

Might now perhaps their wonted impulse give,
Might startle this dull pain, and make it move and
   live!

II

A grief without a pang, void, dark, and drear,
   A stifled, drowsy, unimpassioned grief,
     Which finds no natural outlet, no relief,
       In word, or sigh, or tear –
O Lady! in this wan and heartless mood,
To other thoughts by yonder throstle woo'd,
   All this long eve, so balmy and serene,
Have I been gazing on the western sky,
   And its peculiar tint of yellow green:
And still I gaze – and with how blank an eye!
And those thin clouds above, in flakes and bars,
That give away their motion to the stars;
Those stars, that glide behind them or between,
Now sparkling, now bedimmed, but always seen:
Yon crescent Moon, as fixed as if it grew
In its own cloudless, starless lake of blue;
I see them all so excellently fair,
I see, not feel, how beautiful they are!

III

My genial spirits fail;
And what can these avail
To lift the smothering weight from off my breast?
It were a vain endeavour,
Though I should gaze for ever
On that green light that lingers in the west:
I may not hope from outward forms to win
The passion and the life, whose fountains are within.

IV

O Lady! we receive but what we give,
And in our life alone does Nature live:
Ours is her wedding-garment, ours her shroud!
And would we aught behold, of higher worth,
Than that inanimate cold world allowed
To the poor loveless ever-anxious crowd,
Ah! from the soul itself must issue forth
A light, a glory, a fair luminous cloud
Enveloping the Earth –
And from the soul itself must there be sent
A sweet and potent voice, of its own birth,
Of all sweet sounds the life and element!

V

O pure of heart! thou need'st not ask of me
What this strong music in the soul may be!
What, and wherein it doth exist,
This light, this glory, this fair luminous mist,
This beautiful and beauty-making power.
    Joy, virtuous Lady! Joy that ne'er was given,
Save to the pure, and in their purest hour,
Life, and Life's effluence, cloud at once and shower,
Joy, Lady! is the spirit and the power,
Which wedding Nature to us gives in dower
    A new Earth and new Heaven,
Undreamt of by the sensual and the proud –
Joy is the sweet voice, Joy the luminous cloud –
        We in ourselves rejoice!
And thence flows all that charms or ear or sight,
    All melodies the echoes of that voice,
All colours a suffusion from that light.

VI

There was a time when, though my path was rough,
  This joy within me dallied with distress,
And all misfortunes were but as the stuff
  Whence Fancy made me dreams of happiness:
For hope grew round me, like the twining vine,
And fruits, and foliage, not my own, seemed mine.
But now afflictions bow me down to earth:
Nor care I that they rob me of my mirth,
    But oh! each visitation
Suspends what nature gave me at my birth,
  My shaping spirit of Imagination.
For not to think of what I needs must feel,
  But to be still and patient, all I can;
And haply by abstruse research to steal
  From my own nature all the natural man –
  This was my sole resource, my only plan:
Till that which suits a part infects the whole,
And now is almost grown the habit of my soul.

VII

Hence, viper thoughts, that coil around my mind,
    Reality's dark dream!
I turn from you, and listen to the wind,
  Which long has raved unnoticed. What a scream
Of agony by torture lengthened out
That lute sent forth! Thou Wind, that rav'st without,
  Bare crag, or mountain-tairn, or blasted tree,
Or pine-grove whither woodman never clomb,
Or lonely house, long held the witches' home,
  Methinks were fitter instruments for thee,
Mad Lutanist! who in this month of showers,
Of dark-brown gardens, and of peeping flowers,
Mak'st Devils' yule, with worse than wintry song,
The blossoms, buds, and timorous leaves among.
  Thou Actor, perfect in all tragic sounds!
Thou mighty Poet, e'en to frenzy bold!
    What tell'st thou now about?
    'Tis of the rushing of an host in rout,
  With groans, of trampled men, with smarting
  wounds –
At once they groan with pain, and shudder with the
  cold!
But hush! there is a pause of deepest silence!
  And all that noise, as of a rushing crowd,
With groans, and tremulous shudderings – all is over –
  It tells another tale, with sounds less deep and loud!
    A tale of less affright,
    And tempered with delight,

As Otway's self had framed the tender lay, –
    'Tis of a little child
    Upon a lonesome wild,
Not far from home, but she hath lost her way:
And now moans low in bitter grief and fear,
And now screams loud, and hopes to make her
   mother hear.

VIII

'Tis midnight, but small thoughts have I of sleep:
Full seldom may my friend such vigils keep!
Visit her, gentle Sleep! with wings of healing,
   And may this storm be but a mountain-birth,
May all the stars hang bright above her dwelling,
   Silent as though they watched the sleeping Earth!
      With light heart may she rise,
      Gay fancy, cheerful eyes,
    Joy lift her spirit, joy attune her voice;
To her may all things live, from pole to pole,
Their life the eddying of her living soul!
   O simple spirit, guided from above,
Dear Lady! friend devoutest of my choice,
Thus mayest thou ever, evermore rejoice.

JOHN KEATS
Ode to a Nightingale

1

My heart aches, and a drowsy numbness pains
   My sense, as though of hemlock I had drunk,
Or emptied some dull opiate to the drains
   One minute past, and Lethe-wards had sunk:
'Tis not through envy of thy happy lot,
   But being too happy in thine happiness, –
      That thou, light-winged Dryad of the trees,
         In some melodious plot
Of beechen green, and shadows numberless,
   Singest of summer in full-throated ease.

2

O, for a draught of vintage! that hath been
   Cool'd a long age in the deep-delved earth,
Tasting of Flora and the country green,
   Dance, and Provençal song, and sunburnt mirth!
O for a beaker full of the warm South,
   Full of the true, the blushful Hippocrene,
      With beaded bubbles winking at the brim,
         And purple-stained mouth;
That I might drink, and leave the world unseen,
   And with thee fade away into the forest dim:

3

Fade far away, dissolve, and quite forget
   What thou among the leaves hast never known,
The weariness, the fever, and the fret
   Here, where men sit and hear each other groan;
Where palsy shakes a few, sad, last gray hairs,
     Where youth grows pale, and spectre-thin, and dies;
        Where but to think is to be full of sorrow
          And leaden-eyed despairs,
Where Beauty cannot keep her lustrous eyes,
   Or new Love pine at them beyond to-morrow.

4

Away! away! for I will fly to thee,
   Not charioted by Bacchus and his pards,
But on the viewless wings of Poesy,
   Though the dull brain perplexes and retards:
Already with thee! tender is the night,
     And haply the Queen-Moon is on her throne,
        Cluster'd around by all her starry Fays;
          But here there is no light,
Save what from heaven is with the breezes blown
   Through verdurous glooms and winding mossy
ways.

5

I cannot see what flowers are at my feet,
  Nor what soft incense hangs upon the boughs,
But, in embalmed darkness, guess each sweet
  Wherewith the seasonable month endows
The grass, the thicket, and the fruit-tree wild;
  White hawthorn, and the pastoral eglantine;
    Fast fading violets cover'd up in leaves;
      And mid-May's eldest child,
The coming musk-rose, full of dewy wine,
  The murmurous haunt of flies on summer eves.

6

Darkling I listen; and, for many a time
  I have been half in love with easeful Death,
Call'd him soft names in many a mused rhyme,
  To take into the air my quiet breath;
Now more than ever seems it rich to die,
  To cease upon the midnight with no pain,
    While thou art pouring forth thy soul abroad
      In such an ecstasy!
Still wouldst thou sing, and I have ears in vain –
  To thy high requiem become a sod.

7

Thou wast not born for death, immortal Bird!
   No hungry generations tread thee down;
The voice I hear this passing night was heard
   In ancient days by emperor and clown:
Perhaps the self-same song that found a path
     Through the sad heart of Ruth, when, sick for
     home,
        She stood in tears amid the alien corn;
          The same that oft-times hath
Charm'd magic casements, opening on the foam
    Of perilous seas, in faery lands forlorn.

8

Forlorn! the very word is like a bell
   To toll me back from thee to my sole self!
Adieu! the fancy cannot cheat so well
   As she is fam'd to do, deceiving elf.
Adieu! adieu! thy plaintive anthem fades
   Past the near meadows, over the still stream,
      Up the hill-side; and now 'tis buried deep
        In the next valley-glades:
Was it a vision, or a waking dream?
   Fled is that music: – Do I wake or sleep?

JOHN KEATS
Ode on a Grecian Urn

1

Thou still unravish'd bride of quietness,
    Thou foster-child of silence and slow time,
Sylvan historian, who canst thus express
    A flowery tale more sweetly than our rhyme:
What leaf-fring'd legend haunts about thy shape
    Of deities or mortals, or of both,
        In Tempe or the dales of Arcady?
    What men or gods are these? What maidens loth?
What mad pursuit? What struggle to escape?
        What pipes and timbrels? What wild ecstasy?

2

Heard melodies are sweet, but those unheard
    Are sweeter; therefore, ye soft pipes, play on;
Not to the sensual ear, but, more endear'd,
    Pipe to the spirit ditties of no tone:
Fair youth, beneath the trees, thou canst not leave
    Thy song, nor ever can those trees he bare;
        Bold lover, never, never canst thou kiss,
Though winning near the goal – yet, do not grieve;
        She cannot fade, though thou hast not thy bliss,
    For ever wilt thou love, and she be fair!

3

Ah, happy, happy boughs! that cannot shed
  Your leaves, nor ever bid the spring adieu;
And, happy melodist, unwearied,
  For ever piping songs for ever new;
More happy love! more happy, happy love!
  For ever warm and still to be enjoy'd,
    For ever panting, and for ever young;
All breathing human passion far above,
  That leaves a heart high-sorrowful and cloy'd,
    A burning forehead, and a parching tongue.

4

Who are these coming to the sacrifice?
  To what green altar, O mysterious priest,
Lead'st thou that heifer lowing at the skies,
  And all her silken flanks with garlands drest?
What little town by river or sea shore,
  Or mountain-built with peaceful citadel,
    Is emptied of this folk, this pious morn?
And, little town, thy streets for evermore
  Will silent be; and not a soul to tell
    Why thou art desolate, can e'er return.

O Attic shape! Fair attitude! with brede
  Of marble men and maidens overwrought,
With forest branches and the trodden weed;
  Thou, silent form, dost tease us out of thought
As doth eternity: Cold Pastoral!
  When old age shall this generation waste,
    Thou shalt remain, in midst of other woe
  Than ours, a friend to man, to whom thou say'st,
'Beauty is truth, truth beauty,' – that is all
  Ye know on earth, and all ye need to know.

JOHN KEATS
Ode on Melancholy

1

No, no, go not to Lethe, neither twist
  Wolf's-bane, tight-rooted, for its poisonous wine;
Nor suffer thy pale forehead to be kiss'd
  By nightshade, ruby grape of Proserpine;
Make not your rosary of yew-berries,
  Nor let the beetle, nor the death-moth be
    Your mournful Psyche, nor the downy owl
A partner in your sorrow's mysteries;
  For shade to shade will come too drowsily,
    And drown the wakeful anguish of the soul.

2

But when the melancholy fit shall fall
  Sudden from heaven like a weeping cloud,
That fosters the droop-headed flowers all,
  And hides the green hill in an April shroud;
Then glut thy sorrow on a morning rose,
  Or on the rainbow of the salt sand-wave,
    Or on the wealth of globed peonies;
Or if thy mistress some rich anger shows,
  Emprison her soft hand, and let her rave,
    And feed deep, deep upon her peerless eyes.

3

She dwells with Beauty – Beauty that must die;
  And Joy, whose hand is ever at his lips
Bidding adieu; and aching Pleasure nigh,
  Turning to poison while the bee-mouth sips:
Ay, in the very temple of Delight
  Veil'd Melancholy has her sovran shrine,
    Though seen of none save him whose strenuous
    tongue
  Can burst Joy's grape against his palate fine;
His soul shall taste the sadness of her might,
    And be among her cloudy trophies hung.

JOHN KEATS
Ode to Autumn

1

Season of mists and mellow fruitfulness,
  Close bosom-friend of the maturing sun;
Conspiring with him how to load and bless
  With fruit the vines that round the thatch-eves run;
To bend with apples the moss'd cottage-trees,
  And fill all fruit with ripeness to the core;
    To swell the gourd, and plump the hazel shells
  With a sweet kernel; to set budding more,
And still more, later flowers for the bees,
Until they think warm days will never cease,
    For summer has o'er-brimm'd their clammy cells.

2

Who hath not seen thee oft amid thy store?
  Sometimes whoever seeks abroad may find
Thee sitting careless on a granary floor,
  Thy hair soft-lifted by the winnowing wind;
Or on a half-reap'd furrow sound asleep,
  Drows'd with the fume of poppies, while thy hook
    Spares the next swath and all its twined flowers:
And sometimes like a gleaner thou dost keep
  Steady thy laden head across a brook;
  Or by a cyder-press, with patient look,
    Thou watchest the last oozings hours by hours.

Where are the songs of spring? Ay, where are they?
  Think not of them, thou hast thy music too, –
While barred clouds bloom the soft-dying day,
  And touch the stubble-plains with rosy hue;
Then in a wailful choir the small gnats mourn
  Among the river sallows, borne aloft
    Or sinking as the light wind lives or dies;
And full-grown lambs loud bleat from hilly bourn;
  Hedge-crickets sing; and now with treble soft
  The red-breast whistles from a garden-croft;
    And gathering swallows twitter in the skies.

PERCY BYSSHE SHELLEY
To a Skylark

Hail to thee, blithe Spirit!
 Bird thou never wert,
That from Heaven, or near it,
 Pourest thy full heart
In profuse strains of unpremeditated art.

Higher still and higher
 From the earth thou springest
Like a cloud of fire;
 The blue deep thou wingest,
And singing still dost soar, and soaring ever singest.

In the golden lightning
 Of the sunken sun,
O'er which clouds are bright'ning,
 Thou dost float and run;
Like an unbodied joy whose race is just begun.

The pale purple even
 Melts around thy flight;
Like a star of Heaven,
 In the broad daylight
Thou art unseen, but yet I hear thy shrill delight,

Keen as are the arrows
    Of that silver sphere,
Whose intense lamp narrows
    In the white dawn clear
Until we hardly see – we feel that it is there.

All the earth and air
    With thy voice is loud,
As, when night is bare,
    From one lonely cloud
The moon rains out her beams, and
    Heaven is overflowed.

What thou art we know not;
    What is most like thee?
From rainbow clouds there flow not
    Drops so bright to see
As from thy presence showers a rain of melody.

Like a Poet hidden
    In the light of thought,
Singing hymns unbidden,
    Till the world is wrought
To sympathy with hopes and fears it heeded not:

Like a high-born maiden
    In a palace-tower,
Soothing her love-laden
    Soul in secret hour
With music sweet as love, which overflows her bower:

Like a glow-worm golden
    In a dell of dew,
Scattering unbeholden
    Its aëreal hue
Among the flowers and grass, which screen it from the
    view!

Like a rose embowered
    In its own green leaves,
By warm winds deflowered,
    Till the scent it gives
Makes faint with too much sweet those
    heavy-wingèd thieves:

Sound of vernal showers
    On the twinkling grass,
Rain-awakened flowers,
    All that ever was
Joyous, and clear, and fresh, thy music doth surpass:

Teach us, Sprite or Bird,
    What sweet thoughts are thine:
I have never heard
    Praise of love or wine
That panted forth a flood of rapture so divine.

Chorus Hymeneal,
    Or triumphal chant,
Matched with thine would be all
    But an empty vaunt,
A thing wherein we feel there is some hidden want.

What objects are the fountains
    Of thy happy strain?
What fields, or waves, or mountains?
    What shapes of sky or plain?
What love of thine own kind? what ignorance of pain?

With thy clear keen joyance
    Languor cannot be:
Shadow of annoyance
    Never came near thee:
Thou lovest – but ne'er knew love's sad satiety.

Waking or asleep,
    Thou of death must deem
Things more true and deep
    Than we mortals dream,
Or how could thy notes flow in such a crystal stream?

We look before and after,
    And pine for what is not:
Our sincerest laughter
    With some pain is fraught;
Our sweetest songs are those that tell of saddest
    thought.

Yet if we could scorn
    Hate, and pride, and fear;
If we were things born
    Not to shed a tear,
I know not how thy joy we ever should come near.

Better than all measures
    Of delightful sound,
Better than all treasures
    That in books are found,
Thy skill to poet were, thou scorner of the ground!

Teach me half the gladness
    That thy brain must know,
Such harmonious madness
    From my lips would flow
The world should listen then – as I am listening now.

PERCY BYSSHE SHELLEY
Ode to the West Wind

I

O wild West Wind, thou breath of Autumn's being,
Thou, from whose unseen presence the leaves dead
Are driven, like ghosts from an enchanter fleeing,

Yellow, and black, and pale, and hectic red,
Pestilence-stricken multitudes: O thou,
Who chariotest to their dark wintry bed

The wingèd seeds, where they lie cold and low,
Each like a corpse within its grave, until
Thine azure sister of the Spring shall blow

Her clarion o'er the dreaming earth, and fill
(Driving sweet buds like flocks to feed in air)
With living hues and odours plain and hill:

Wild Spirit, which art moving everywhere;
Destroyer and preserver; hear, oh, hear!

II

Thou on whose stream, mid the steep sky's
   commotion,
Loose clouds like earth's decaying leaves are shed,
Shook from the tangled boughs of Heaven and Ocean,

Angels of rain and lightning: there are spread
On the blue surface of thine aëry surge,
Like the bright hair uplifted from the head

Of some fierce Maenad, even from the dim verge
Of the horizon to the zenith's height,
The locks of the approaching storm. Thou dirge

Of the dying year, to which this closing night
Will be the dome of a vast sepulchre,
Vaulted with all thy congregated might

Of vapours, from whose solid atmosphere
Black rain, and fire, and hail will burst: oh, hear!

III

Thou who didst waken from his summer dreams
The blue Mediterranean, where he lay,
Lulled by the coil of his crystàlline streams,

Beside a pumice isle in Baiae's bay,
And saw in sleep old palaces and towers
Quivering within the wave's intenser day,

All overgrown with azure moss and flowers
So sweet, the sense faints picturing them! Thou
For whose path the Atlantic's level powers

Cleave themselves into chasms, while far below
The sea-blooms and the oozy woods which wear
The sapless foliage of the ocean, know

Thy voice, and suddenly grow gray with fear,
And tremble and despoil themselves: oh, hear!

IV

If I were a dead leaf thou mightest bear;
If I were a swift cloud to fly with thee;
A wave to pant beneath thy power, and share

The impulse of thy strength, only less free
Than thou, O uncontrollable! If even
I were as in my boyhood, and could be

The comrade of thy wanderings over Heaven,
As then, when to outstrip thy skiey speed
Scarce seemed a vision; I would ne'er have striven

As thus with thee in prayer in my sore need.
Oh, lift me as a wave, a leaf, a cloud!
I fall upon the thorns of life! I bleed!

A heavy weight of hours has chained and bowed
One too like thee: tameless, and swift, and proud.

V

Make me thy lyre, even as the forest is:
What if my leaves are falling like its own!
The tumult of thy mighty harmonies

Will take from both a deep, autumnal tone,
Sweet though in sadness. Be thou, Spirit fierce,
My spirit! Be thou me, impetuous one!

Drive my dead thoughts over the universe
Like withered leaves to quicken a new birth!
And, by the incantation of this verse,

Scatter, as from an unextinguished hearth
Ashes and sparks, my words among mankind!
Be through my lips to unawakened earth

The trumpet of a prophecy! O, Wind,
If Winter comes, can Spring be far behind?

PERCY BYSSHE SHELLEY
From Ode to Liberty

Oh, that the free would stamp the impious name
   Of King into the dust! or write it there,
So that this blot upon the page of fame
   Were as a serpent's path, which the light air
Erases, and the flat sands close behind!
         Ye the oracle have heard:
         Lift the victory-flashing sword,
And cut the snaky knots of this foul gordian word,
   Which, weak itself as stubble, yet can bind
      Into a mass, irrefragably firm,
   The axes and the rods which awe mankind;
      The sound has poison in it, 'tis the sperm
Of what makes life foul, cankerous, and abhorred;
   Disdain not thou, at thine appointed term,
   To set thine armèd heel on this reluctant worm.

Oh, that the wise from their bright minds would kindle
   Such lamps within the dome of this dim world,
That the pale name of Priest might shrink and dwindle
   Into the hell from which it first was hurled,
A scoff of impious pride from fiends impure;
         Till human thoughts might kneel alone,
         Each before the judgement-throne
Of its own aweless soul, or of the Power unknown!
   Oh, that the words which make the thoughts obscure
      From which they spring, as clouds of glimmering dew

82

From a white lake blot Heaven's blue portraiture,
    Were stripped of their thin masks and various hue
And frowns and smiles and splendours not their own,
    Till in the nakedness of false and true
    They stand before their Lord, each to receive its due!

He who taught man to vanquish whatsoever
    Can be between the cradle and the grave
Crowned him the King of Life. Oh, vain endeavour!
    If on his own high will, a willing slave,
He has enthroned the oppression and the oppressor.
        What if earth can clothe and feed
        Amplest millions at their need,
And power in thought be as the tree within the seed?
    Or what if Art, an ardent intercessor,
        Driving on fiery wings to Nature's throne,
Checks the great mother stooping to caress her,
        And cries: 'Give me, thy child, dominion
Over all height and depth'? if Life can breed
    New wants, and wealth from those who toil and groan
Rend of thy gifts and hers a thousandfold for one!

Come thou, but lead out of the inmost cave
    Of man's deep spirit, as the morning-star
Beckons the Sun from the Eoan wave,
    Wisdom. I hear the pennons of her car
Self-moving, like cloud charioted by flame;
        Comes she not, and come ye not,
        Rulers of eternal thought,

To judge, with solemn truth, life's ill-apportioned lot?
  Blind Love, and equal Justice, and the Fame
    Of what has been, the Hope of what will be?
  O Liberty! if such could be thy name
    Wert thou disjoined from these, or they from
  thee:
If thine or theirs were treasures to be bought
  By blood or tears, have not the wise and free
  Wept tears, and blood like tears? – The solemn
  harmony

Paused, and the Spirit of that mighty singing
  To its abyss was suddenly withdrawn;
Then, as a wild swan, when sublimely winging
  Its path athwart the thunder-smoke of dawn,
Sinks headlong through the aëreal golden light
    On the heavy-sounding plain,
    When the bolt has pierced its brain;
As summer clouds dissolve, unburthened of their rain;
  As a far taper fades with fading night,
    As a brief insect dies with dying day, –
  My song, its pinions disarrayed of might,
    Drooped; o'er it closed the echoes far away
Of the great voice which did its flight sustain,
  As waves which lately paved his watery way
  Hiss round a drowner's head in their tempestuous
  play.

ALFRED TENNYSON
Ode on the Death of the Duke of Wellington

I

Bury the Great Duke
  With an empire's lamentation,
Let us bury the Great Duke
  To the noise of the mourning of a mighty
  nation,
Mourning when their leaders fall,
Warriors carry the warrior's pall,
And sorrow darkens hamlet and hall.

II

Where shall we lay the man whom we deplore?
Here, in streaming London's central roar.
Let the sound of those he wrought for,
And the feet of those he fought for,
Echo round his bones for evermore.

III

Lead out the pageant: sad and slow,
As fits an universal woe,
Let the long long procession go,
And let the sorrowing crowd about it grow,
And let the mournful martial music blow;
The last great Englishman is low.

Mourn, for to us he seems the last,
Remembering all his greatness in the Past.
No more in soldier fashion will he greet
With lifted hand the gazer in the street.
O friends, our chief state-oracle is mute:
Mourn for the man of long-enduring blood,
The statesman-warrior, moderate, resolute,
Whole in himself, a common good.
Mourn for the man of amplest influence,
Yet clearest of ambitious crime,
Our greatest yet with least pretence,
Great in council and great in war,
Foremost captain of his time,
Rich in saving common-sense,
And, as the greatest only are,
In his simplicity sublime.
O good gray head which all men knew,
O voice from which their omens all men drew,
O iron nerve to true occasion true,
O fall'n at length that tower of strength
Which stood four-square to all the winds that blew!
Such was he whom we deplore.
The long self-sacrifice of life is o'er.
The great World-victor's victor will be seen no
    more.

V

All is over and done:
Render thanks to the Giver,
England, for thy son.
Let the bell be toll'd.
Render thanks to the Giver,
And render him to the mould.
Under the cross of gold
That shines over city and river,
There he shall rest for ever
Among the wise and the bold.
Let the bell be toll'd:
And a reverent people behold
The towering car, the sable steeds:
Bright let it be with its blazon'd deeds,
Dark in its funeral fold.
Let the bell be toll'd:
And a deeper knell in the heart be knoll'd;
And the sound of the sorrowing anthem roll'd
Thro' the dome of the golden cross;
And the volleying cannon thunder his loss;
He knew their voices of old.
For many a time in many a clime
His captain's-ear has heard them boom
Bellowing victory, bellowing doom:
When he with those deep voices wrought,
Guarding realms and kings from shame;
With those deep voices our dead captain taught
The tyrant, and asserts his claim

What though the music of thy rustic flute
   Kept not for long its happy, country tone;
      Lost it too soon, and learnt a stormy note
Of men contention-tost, of men who groan,
     Which task'd thy pipe too sore, and tired thy
        throat –
       It fail'd, and thou wast mute!
Yet hadst thou alway visions of our light,
    And long with men of care thou couldst not stay,
    And soon thy foot resumed its wandering way,
Left human haunt, and on alone till night.

Too rare, too rare, grow now my visits here!
   'Mid city-noise, not, as with thee of yore,
     Thyrsis! in reach of sheep-bells is my home.
   – Then through the great town's harsh,
       heart-wearying roar,
    Let in thy voice a whisper often come,
      To chase fatigue and fear:
  Why faintest thou? I wander'd till I died.
  Roam on! The light we sought is shining still.
  Dost thou ask proof? Our tree yet crowns the hill,
Our Scholar travels yet the loved hill-side.

THOMAS HARDY
The Going

Why did you give no hint that night
That quickly after the morrow's dawn,
And calmly, as if indifferent quite,
You would close your term here, up and be gone
   Where I could not follow
   With wing of swallow
To gain one glimpse of you ever anon!

   Never to bid good-bye,
   Or lip me the softest call,
Or utter a wish for a word, while I
Saw morning harden upon the wall,
   Unmoved, unknowing
   That your great going
Had place that moment, and altered all.

Why do you make me leave the house
And think for a breath it is you I see
At the end of the alley of bending boughs
Where so often at dusk you used to be;
   Till in darkening dankness
   The yawning blankness
Of the perspective sickens me!

Their surging charges foam'd themselves away;
Last, the Prussian trumpet blew;
Thro' the long-tormented air
Heaven flash'd a sudden jubilant ray,
And down we swept and charged and overthrew.
So great a soldier taught us there,
What long-enduring hearts could do
In that world-earthquake, Waterloo!
Mighty Seaman, tender and true,
And pure as he from taint of craven guile,
O saviour of the silver-coasted isle,
O shaker of the Baltic and the Nile,
If aught of things that here befall
Touch a spirit among things divine,
If love of country move thee there at all,
Be glad, because his bones are laid by thine!
And thro' the centuries let a people's voice
In full acclaim,
A people's voice,
The proof and echo of all human fame,
A people's voice, when they rejoice
At civic revel and pomp and game,
Attest their great commander's claim
With honour, honour, honour, honour to him,
Eternal honour to his name.

VII

A people's voice! we are a people yet.
Tho' all men else their nobler dreams forget,
Confused by brainless mobs and lawless Powers;
Thank Him who isled us here, and roughly set
His Briton in blown seas and storming showers,
We have a voice, with which to pay the debt
Of boundless love and reverence and regret,
To those great men who fought, and kept it ours.
And keep it ours, O God, from brute control;
O Statesmen, guard us, guard the eye, the soul
Of Europe, keep our noble England whole,
And save the one true seed of freedom sown
Betwixt a people and their ancient throne,
That sober freedom out of which there springs
Our loyal passion for our temperate kings;
For, saving that, ye help to save mankind
Till public wrong be crumbled into dust,
And drill the raw world for the march of mind,
Till crowds at length be sane and crowns be just.
But wink no more in slothful overtrust.
Remember him who led your hosts;
He bad you guard the sacred coasts.
Your cannons moulder on the seaward wall;
His voice is silent in your council-hall
For ever; and whatever tempests lour
For ever silent; even if they broke
In thunder, silent; yet remember all
He spoke among you, and the Man who spoke;

Who never sold the truth to serve the hour,
Nor palter'd with Eternal God for power;
Who let the turbid streams of rumour flow
Thro' either babbling world of high and low;
Whose life was work, whose language rife
With rugged maxims hewn from life;
Who never spoke against a foe;
Whose eighty winters freeze with one rebuke
All great self-seekers trampling on the right:
Truth-teller was our England's Alfred named;
Truth-lover was our English Duke;
Whatever record leap to light
He never shall be shamed.

VIII

Lo, the leader in these glorious wars
Now to glorious burial slowly borne,
Follow'd by the brave of other lands,
He, on whom from both her open hands
Lavish Honour shower'd all her stars,
And affluent Fortune emptied all her horn.
Yea, let all good things await
Him who cares not to be great,
But as he saves or serves the state.
Not once or twice in our rough island-story,
The path of duty was the way to glory:
He that walks it, only thirsting
For the right, and learns to deaden
Love of self, before his journey closes,

He shall find the stubborn thistle bursting
Into glossy purples, which outredden
All voluptuous garden-roses.
Not once or twice in our fair island-story,
The path of duty was the way to glory:
He, that ever following her commands,
On with toil of heart and knees and hands,
Thro' the long gorge to the far light has won
His path upward, and prevail'd,
Shall find the toppling crags of Duty scaled
Are close upon the shining table-lands
To which our God Himself is moon and sun.
Such was he: his work is done.
But while the races of mankind endure,
Let his great example stand
Colossal, seen of every land,
And keep the soldier firm, the statesman pure:
Till in all lands and thro' all human story
The path of duty be the way to glory:
And let the land whose hearths he saved from shame
For many and many an age proclaim
At civic revel and pomp and game,
And when the long-illumined cities flame,
Their ever-loyal iron leader's fame,
With honour, honour, honour, honour to him,
Eternal honour to his name.

IX

Peace, his triumph will be sung
By some yet unmoulded tongue
Far on in summers that we shall not see:
Peace, it is a day of pain
For one about whose patriarchal knee
Late the little children clung:
O peace, it is a day of pain
For one, upon whose hand and heart and brain
Once the weight and fate of Europe hung.
Ours the pain, be his the gain!
More than is of man's degree
Must be with us, watching here
At this, our great solemnity.
Whom we see not we revere;
We revere, and we refrain
From talk of battles loud and vain,
And brawling memories all too free
For such a wise humility
As befits a solemn fane:
We revere, and while we hear
The tides of Music's golden sea
Setting toward eternity,
Uplifted high in heart and hope are we,
Until we doubt not that for one so true
There must be other nobler work to do
Than when he fought at Waterloo,
And Victor he must ever be.
For tho' the Giant Ages heave the hill

And break the shore, and evermore
Make and break, and work their will;
Tho' world on world in myriad myriads roll
Round us, each with different powers,
And other forms of life than ours,
What know we greater than the soul?
On God and Godlike men we build our trust.
Hush, the Dead March wails in the people's ears:
The dark crowd moves, and there are sobs and
　　tears:
The black earth yawns: the mortal disappears;
Ashes to ashes, dust to dust;
He is gone who seem'd so great. –
Gone; but nothing can bereave him
Of the force he made his own
Being here, and we believe him
Something far advanced in State,
And that he wears a truer crown
Than any wreath that man can weave him.
Speak no more of his renown,
Lay your earthly fancies down,
And in the vast cathedral leave him.
God accept him, Christ receive him.